# Floods, Dams, and Levees

By Joanne Mattern

ROAD
FLOODED

ROURKE
PUBLISHING

www.rourkepublishing.com

www.rourkepublishing.com

PHOTO CREDITS: Front Cover: © Colin Stitt; © Marivlada; © Vladimir Melnikov, Back Cover: © ArtShare.ru; Title page © samotrebizan, Timothy Large, Melissa Brandes; Table of contents ©  kor; Page 4/5 © Christian Vinces, Page 4 © manit321, Page 5 © Jerry Sharp; Page 6 © Alyssia Sheik, NOAA; Page 7 © Ed Edahl/FEMA; Page 8/9 © Timothy Large; Page 9 © Melissa Brandes, Casper Simon; Page 10 © Caitlin Mirra; Page 11 © Feng Yu; Page 12/13 © Wessel du Plooy; Page 12 © ASSOCIATED PRESS, AARON RHOADS; Page 14/15 © NASA; Page 15 © Styve Reineck; Page 16/17 © Ramon Berk; Page 16 © pio3; Page 17 © B.L. Singley; Page 18/19 © Paco Espinoza; Page 19 © ChiefHira; Page 20 © Roland Zihlmann; Page 21 © Alyssia Sheikh; Page 22 © Iafoto; Page 23 © Foto011; Page 24/25 © elwynn; Page 25 © Mikhail Markovskiy; Page 26/27 © Tony Campbell; Page 27 © US Army Corps of Engineers; Page 28 © Volina; Page 29 ©  Iafoto, Charly Morlock www.charlymorlock.com; Page 30/31 ©  Igor Grochev; Page 31 © U.S. Army Corps of Engineers; Page 32 © Christian Lopetz; Page 33 © NOAA; Page 34 © Exactostock/SuperStock; Page 35 © Dean Kerr, NOAA; Page 36 © NASA; Page 37 © Carolina K. Smith, M.D.; Page 38 © NOAA; Page 39 © Marcel Jancovic; Page 40 © rgerhardt; Page 41 © NOAA; Page 43 © Markus Gebauer / Shutterstock.com; Page 44 © Monkey Business Images; Page 45 © egd

Edited by Precious McKenzie

Cover design by Teri Intzegian
Layout by Blue Door Publishing, FL

### Library of Congress Cataloging-in-Publication Data

Mattern, Joanne
  Floods, Dams, and Levees / Joanne Mattern
    p. cm. --  (Let's Explore Science)
  ISBN 978-1-61741-786-3 (hard cover) (alk. paper)
  ISBN 978-1-61741-988-1 (soft cover)
  Library of Congress Control Number:  2011924831

Rourke Publishing
Printed in the United States of America, North Mankato, Minnesota
060711
060711CL

www.rourkepublishing.com - rourke@rourkepublishing.com
Post Office Box 643328 Vero Beach, Florida 32964

# Table of Contents

# CHAPTER ONE

# What Is a Flood?

Water is one of the most powerful forces on Earth. When water is controlled, it can help people in many ways. Water can move machinery and create energy. It can move boats and barges, carrying people and goods all over the world. People could not survive without water to drink and to nourish plants and animals.

Sometimes, however, water gets out of control. When this happens, an area can suffer a flood. A flood occurs when water covers an area that is usually dry. Most floods happen naturally. A river, lake, or other body of water may overflow because of too much rain or melting snow. Or a bad storm can dump several inches of rain on an area, filling streets and homes and causing waterways to spill over.

Other floods are manmade. People might build a dam that is not strong enough to hold back water. Or a dam can be damaged and break, releasing the water behind it.

The flood in Johnstown destroyed four square miles (10 kilometers) of the city's downtown and 1,600 houses.

In 1889, Johnstown, Pennsylvania, received several inches of rain. The rain was too much for the South Fork Dam, which stood about 12 miles (19.3 kilometers) above Johnstown. The dam collapsed, sending a wall of water down the river. The water reached 75 feet (23 meters) high and was powerful enough to wash away train locomotives. Johnstown was destroyed by the flood, and more than 2,000 people were killed.

Some floods take a long time to develop. A storm might last for days, causing rivers and streams to rise over time. After a few days, the water rises over the banks of the river and floods the land around it. Melting snow can also fill rivers and other bodies of water until they flood. **Meteorologists** can often warn people so they can protect their homes and get to safety if they have to.

### Did You Know?

Sometimes areas that do not have a history of flooding begin to flood. Often, this is the result of new land development that changes the natural runoff paths.

Some floods happen very quickly. This type of disaster is called a flash flood. Flash floods usually happen after a heavy rainstorm or a thunderstorm. The rain falls so hard and fast that the ground cannot absorb it. Flash floods are very dangerous because people have very little warning or time to escape.

## Did You Know?

Floods can even happen in the desert! The ground in a desert is usually very dry and hard, so it can't absorb rain from a heavy downpour.

The floodwaters from Hurricane Katrina destroyed most of New Orleans and the surrounding area. About 80 percent of New Orleans flooded.

During a flood, the water can rise very quickly. It can fill streets, making it impossible for people to drive. People may be stranded in their cars during a flood. Flood waters can also enter homes and businesses. Flood waters can destroy property and buildings. A powerful flood can move furniture around a room and knock holes in the walls.

Flood waters can destroy the electrical system in a house and even cause a fire. Floods can fill a house with mud and **debris** which must be cleaned up. Water can also cause mold to form in a building. Mold can cause many serious illnesses.

Floods are very dangerous. Even people who know how to swim can be swept away by a flood's raging waters. People can also be injured or killed if they are hit by debris in the water. Flood waters can also be filled with dangerous chemicals and even dangerous animals, such as snakes and crocodiles!

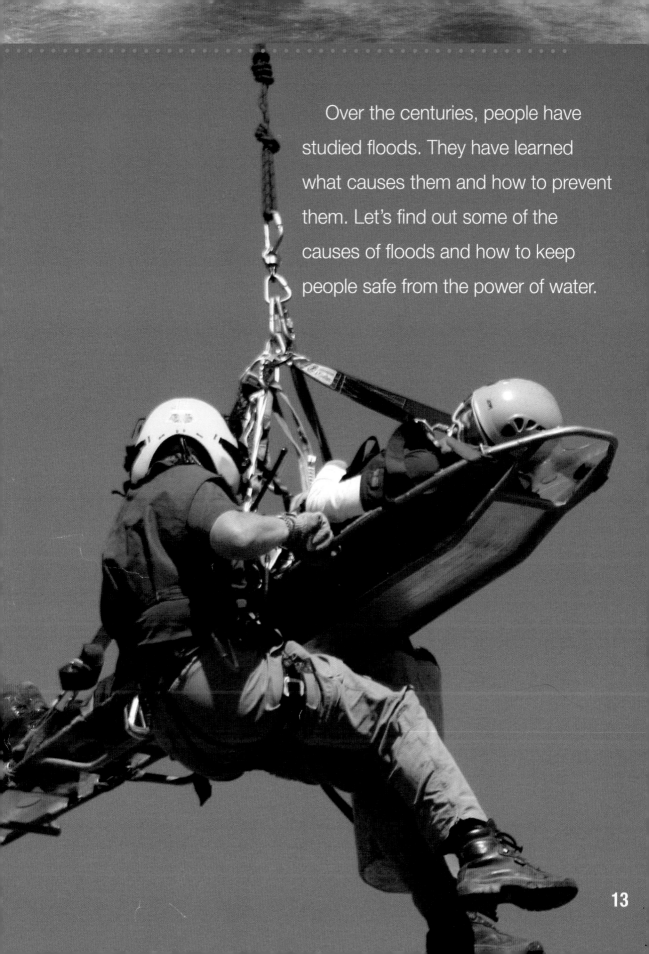

Over the centuries, people have studied floods. They have learned what causes them and how to prevent them. Let's find out some of the causes of floods and how to keep people safe from the power of water.

# CHAPTER TWO

# The Causes Of Floods

There are many events that can cause a flood. One of the most common is a storm. Rainstorms occur all the time, and usually don't cause floods. When it rains, the water flows into streams, rivers, and other bodies of water. From there, the water eventually flows into a larger body of water, such as a lake or the ocean. Usually storms are fairly mild, and not much rain falls. Rivers and streams usually have no problem taking in small amounts of water.

If there is a heavy rain, the area around a stream, river, or lake might become flooded. An area of low-lying, flat land next to a body of water is called a **floodplain**. Even if a floodplain ends up under water, the water usually drains back into the river or stream after a short time, with little damage done. However, if there are buildings or other manmade structures in the floodplain, they can be damaged by the rising water.

## Did You Know?

Floods are not always harmful! Flood waters leave behind rich mud that is filled with minerals and other nutrients. For many years, farmers along the Nile River in Egypt relied on that river's annual flood to enrich the soil and provide a good place for growing crops.

**Tropical cyclones**, also called **hurricanes** or **typhoons**, are a major cause of flooding. These storms can produce more than a foot (30 centimeters) of rain in a day. Tropical cyclones also have strong winds. These winds create huge waves in the ocean, which can flood surrounding communities. Wind can also whip up the water in a lake, causing it to overflow its banks.

**Storm surges** are another type of dangerous flood. Storm surges happen during hurricanes and typhoons. During these storms, an area of low **air pressure** moves over a part of an ocean. This low pressure causes the surface of the ocean to rise. When a hurricane passes over coastal land, the rising water rushes over the land, causing a flood that can stretch for miles.

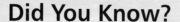

## Did You Know?

All hurricanes and typhoons are tropical cyclones. When a tropical cyclone forms in the Atlantic Ocean, the northeast Pacific Ocean, or the south Pacific Ocean it's called a hurricane. But if a tropical cyclone forms in the northwest Pacific Ocean, it is called a typhoon.

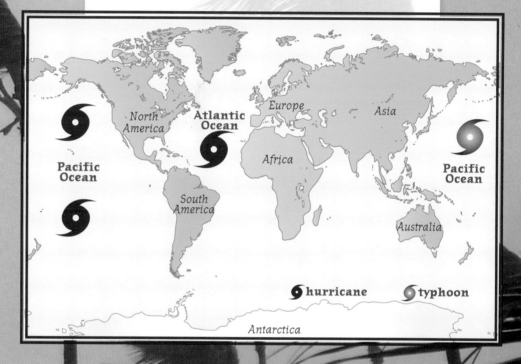

The deadliest natural disaster in U.S. history occurred during a hurricane and storm surge that struck Galveston, Texas, in 1900. More than 6,000 people were killed when 15-foot (4.5 meter)

Some floods are caused by huge waves. A **tsunami** is a series of giant ocean waves. Tsunamis are most common in the Pacific Ocean. They often occur after earthquakes or volcanic eruptions. During a tsunami, waves build up into a giant wall of water that can be up to 100 feet (30 meters) high. When this wave reaches land, it floods everything in its path. In 2004, a tsunami in the Indian Ocean sent 50-foot (15 meter) waves sweeping over Indonesia, Thailand, Sri Lanka, and India. More than 230,000 people were killed and some towns and villages were wiped right off the map.

On March 11, 2011, a powerful earthquake in the Pacific Ocean off the coast of Japan caused a devastating tsunami. Some of the waves from the tsunami traveled 6 miles (10 kilometers) inland.

Melting snow also causes flooding. As snow melts in the mountains, it flows into streams and rivers. If a lot of snow melts in a short time, rivers and streams can be overwhelmed and overflow their banks.

North Dakota

Wisconsin

South Dakota

Minnesota

Michigan

Iowa

Nebraska

Ohio

Illinois

Indiana

Kansas

Missouri

Kentucky

Mississippi River

## Did You Know?

The Mississippi River has had many floods caused by heavy snowmelt combined with severe spring rainstorms. In 1993, the area received rain almost every day for two months. Rivers stayed above flood level from May to September and affected ten states. More than 75,000 people had to leave their homes during the disaster.

In the spring of 2011, heavy rains and snow melt again caused flooding along the Mississippi from Minnesota to the Gulf of Mexico.

Tennessee

Arkansas

Georgi

Mississippi River

Mississippi

Alabama

Louisiana

Texas

*Gulf of Mexico*  21

Dams are just one way humans control the power of water.

Objects built by people can also cause floods. Over the years, people have built many **dams** to block or control the flow of water. A large lake forms behind the walls of the dam. All this water puts a lot of pressure on the walls. Sometimes, the pressure is too much and the dam cracks or breaks. When this happens, a huge flood of water can rush downstream, destroying everything in its path.

**Aerial view of a water barrier dam in Perucac, Serbia.**

Engineers monitor the strength of dams and levees in order to protect the surrounding areas from flooding.

People create flood damage in another way. They often build homes too close to the water. At one time, many rivers were surrounded by marshes or empty fields. These areas acted as a floodplain and absorbed the water from a flood without any people or property getting in the way. In recent years, however, people have built homes and businesses along riverbanks, lakes, and coastlines. As a result, when a natural event like a flood or tropical cyclone occurs, the damage can be much worse than it would have been years earlier when the land was still undeveloped.

### Did You Know?

Waterfront property is worth 8 to 45 percent more than similar inland property.

# CHAPTER THREE

# Controlling the Water

People have been trying to control water since before recorded history. One way they have done this is by building dams and **levees**.

A levee is a raised riverbank. A levee can be naturally made, such as a bank of earth. Or it can be artificially made by **engineers**. Artificial levees are usually made of sandbags or earth. Sandbags work because the sand inside them becomes hard when it absorbs water, creating an artificial wall.

People often fish or hike around levees.

Some levees control the water for farmers and their surrounding fields or protect cities from rising river waters.

Like a levee, a dam can also be natural or artificially made. Dams block the flow of water. Water is trapped behind the dam, forming a pond or a lake. Dams can be useful for preventing floods. They are also used to create **reservoirs** for drinking water and to manage water used to create **hydroelectric power.**

The first dam that historians know about was built on the Nile River in ancient Egypt more than 5,000 years ago. This dam was nearly 350 feet (106 meters) wide and was made of stones and gravel. However, the dam was not well made and it washed away after a few years.

Europe

Africa

Italy

Rome

Nile

Egypt

Nile

The ancient Romans were excellent dam builders. Instead of using dirt and rocks, the ancient Romans built their dams of concrete. These dams were much stronger and worked well to control the flow of water.

**Embankment Dam**

Ancient dams were called embankment dams or gravity dams. These dams worked because they were so wide and thick that the water could not get past them. Later, during the thirteenth century, Europeans invented the arch dam. This type of dam has a curved shape which makes the dam more stable. An arch dam's walls do not have to be as thick as a gravity dam's to hold back water.

**Arch Dam**

Modern dams are amazing feats of engineering. Modern dams include channels or **spillways** that open to safely release extra water. These channels drain water into pools where it remains until the water level in the river has gone down. Then the water in the pool drains back into the river, where it flows safely downstream.

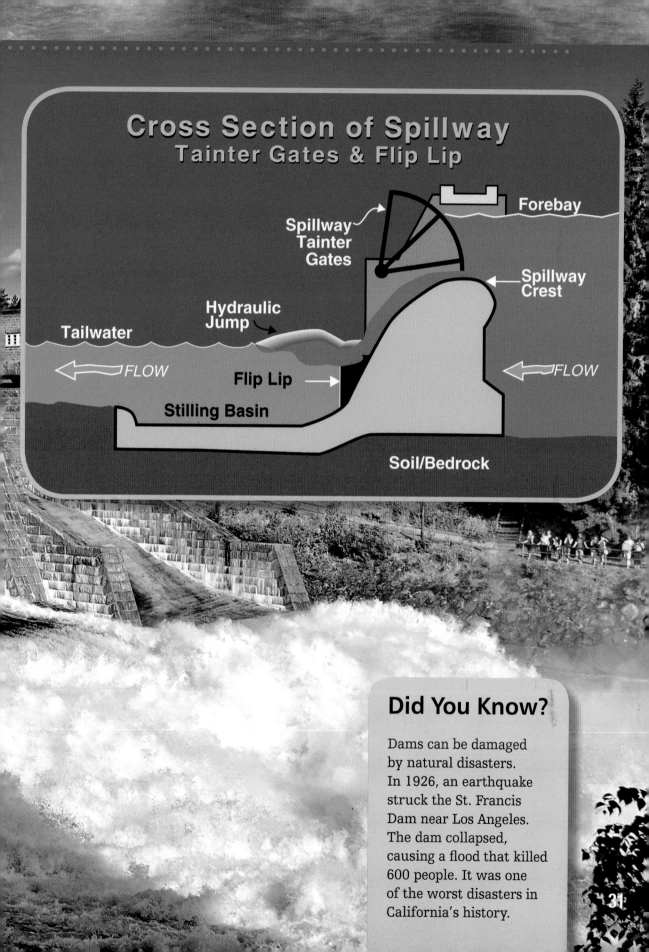

# Cross Section of Spillway
## Tainter Gates & Flip Lip

Forebay

Spillway Tainter Gates

Spillway Crest

Hydraulic Jump

Tailwater

FLOW

Flip Lip

FLOW

Stilling Basin

Soil/Bedrock

## Did You Know?

Dams can be damaged by natural disasters. In 1926, an earthquake struck the St. Francis Dam near Los Angeles. The dam collapsed, causing a flood that killed 600 people. It was one of the worst disasters in California's history.

31

Levees, or dikes, have also been used for thousands of years to control flooding. The ancient Egyptians and Sumerians used levees to control river flooding about 3,000 years ago.

Levees are an important tool to keep rivers under control. They can also be used to protect land from ocean flooding. One of the most famous levee systems in the world is located in the Netherlands. Much of the Netherlands is at sea level or below, and the nation has suffered some devastating floods. Today, thousands of miles of levees protect the Netherlands and keep the nation from being flooded.

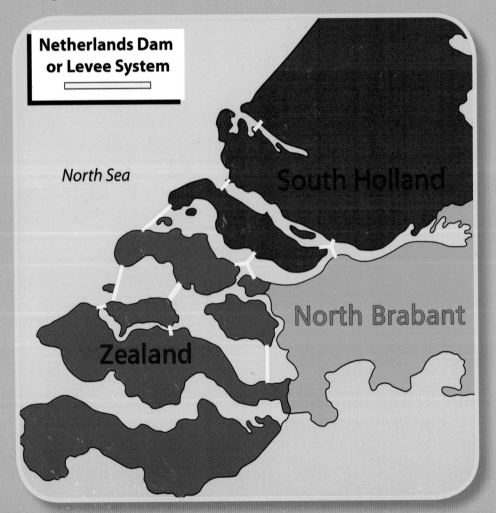

**Netherlands Dam or Levee System**

North Sea

South Holland

North Brabant

Zealand

However, levees do not always work. The levees did not protect the city of New Orleans during Hurricane Katrina in August 2005. During the storm, several levees broke, and New Orleans and its residents were devastated by flood waters.

## Did You Know?

After a terrible flood in 1927, the U.S. government began building levees along the Mississippi River. Today, more than 1,500 levees protect about 27,000 square miles (43,000 kilometers) of land along the river.

# CHAPTER FOUR

# People Who Help

Many people study weather, water, and their effects on the environment. Let's meet some of the people who have made floods a big part of their lives.

Meteorologists are scientists who study the weather. Meteorologists use computer models, **radar**, and other technology to study weather patterns and make predictions about upcoming storms and other weather conditions. They also study images from weather **satellites**.

Meteorologists warn people about dangerous weather systems.

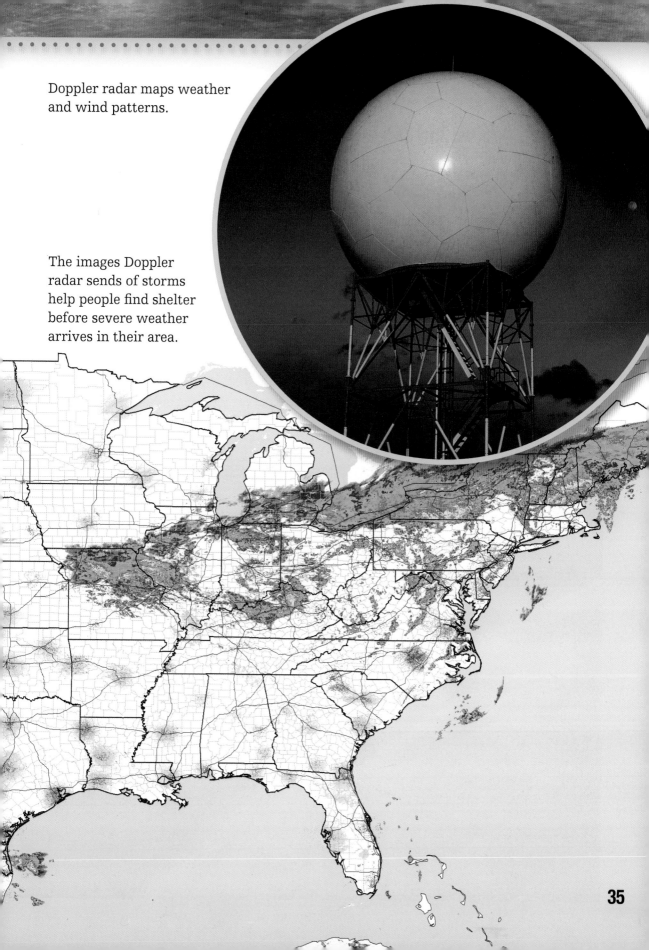

Doppler radar maps weather and wind patterns.

The images Doppler radar sends of storms help people find shelter before severe weather arrives in their area.

Weather satellites orbit the Earth, taking pictures of the planet and its **atmosphere**. These images are sent to weather stations on the ground, where meteorologists study them and use the information to predict weather patterns. These satellite pictures can show storms and other weather patterns developing thousands of miles away, and allow scientists to figure out how the storms will move and affect areas in the future.

NOAA's environmental satellites are the primary source of data that the National Weather Service uses to create the weather forecasts that we hear on television or read on the Internet.

Weather satellites use cloud temperatures to determine severity of storms.

For example, a tropical storm might form far out in the Atlantic Ocean. Meteorologists can study wind patterns and atmospheric pressure to predict that this faraway storm could turn into a hurricane that could cause flooding along the eastern coast of the United States ten days later.

Meteorologists sometimes risk their lives tracking storms to protect people.

Radar is another important tool for meteorologists. Meteorologists can use radar to track the path of a storm and make predictions about where it will go next. They can figure out what areas might receive heavy rain and alert officials and other residents that flooding might occur.

Computer models figure out how much water the soil of a floodplain can absorb. This information lets meteorologists know that a heavy rainstorm or snowmelt could cause more water to flow into an area than the soil can handle, and that flooding is likely to occur.

## Did You Know?

Flash floods are hard to predict, but scientists are working on ways to change that. The Tropical Rainfall Measuring Mission satellite can see how much moisture is in the soil. This information warns meteorologists that an area could flood if thunderstorms or other heavy downpours are predicted.

While meteorologists predict and track the weather, engineers work to prevent and control flooding. Engineers design dams and levees in an effort to control and even change the flow of water. These scientists use precise mechanical and mathematical formulas to figure out how a dam or levee should be shaped, how heavy and high it should be, and exactly where it should be placed to best control a raging river or ocean waves.

## Did You Know?

The United States Army Corps of Engineers is one of the most important groups working to prevent floods. The Corps is a federal agency and an Army command made up of about 34,000 civilian and military personnel. The Corps works on public engineering projects, including the design, construction, and management of dams and canals in the United States.

After a dam or levee is built, people are needed to monitor and control it. Operators measure the water level and release water through spillways if necessary. Safety inspectors also check dams and levees for cracks or weak areas that could collapse.

Despite the best efforts of meteorologists, scientists, and engineers, floods do happen. During and after a flood, emergency workers are ready to help people in trouble. Many firefighters and police officers are trained to do water rescue. Other emergency agencies, such as the Red Cross, work to find shelter, medical care, and supplies for people who have lost their homes and belongings to raging flood waters.

Without the tireless work of emergency personnel, many more lives would be lost during natural disasters.

# CHAPTER FIVE

# Staying Safe

When rivers, lakes, or oceans flood, disaster can happen. Millions of people have lost their homes and their possessions to floods over the years, and many lives have been lost. Fortunately, there are ways people can protect themselves and stay safe during a flood.

The best way to prevent flood damage is to be prepared. If a storm threatens, meteorologists release warnings on television, radio, and the Internet. People should listen to these warnings and follow instructions.

Residents should prepare for storms before they happen, especially in areas that are likely to flood. Homes should have an emergency kit that includes flashlights, a battery-powered weather radio, bottled water, canned food, first aid supplies, and blankets.

## Did You Know?

A flood watch means that conditions are right for a flood to occur. A flood warning is more serious. It means that serious flooding will occur, or might even have started already.

Sandbags may prevent some water from getting into homes but they are not foolproof.

If a flood is predicted for your area, move valuable items to a second floor or attic if possible. You should also bring in any outdoor objects, such as furniture or garbage pails. Stay inside during a flood, unless your area is told to **evacuate**. If you do evacuate, leave enough time to get to shelter before conditions get too bad to travel.

Being outside in a flood is very dangerous. Do not walk, swim, or drive in flooded areas. Water can be deeper than it appears, or it could contain hidden dangers such as downed power lines, toxic chemicals, or heavy debris.

Floods are very dangerous and scary, but if you follow instructions and use common sense, you have a much better chance of surviving nature's fury!

## Did You Know?

It doesn't take a lot of water to be dangerous. Just 6 inches (15 centimeters) of fast-moving water can knock over a person. Just 2 feet (61 centimeters) of water can carry away a car.

# Glossary

**air pressure** (AIR PRESH-ur): the weight of air pressing down on Earth's surface

**atmosphere** (at-muhss-fihr): the layer of gases surrounding Earth

**dams** (DAMZ): structures that block the flow of water

**debris** (duh-BREE): pieces of something that has been destroyed or broken

**engineers** (en-juh-NIHRZ): people who are trained to design and build machines or structures

**evacuate** (i-VAK-yoo-ate): to leave an area because of an emergency

**floodplain** (FLUHD-plane): an area of low-lying, flat land next to a body of water

**hurricanes** (HUR-uh-kanez): tropical storms in the Atlantic Ocean, Caribbean Sea, and the Gulf of Mexico that produce high winds and heavy rains

**hydroelectric power** (hy-droh-i-LEK-trik POU-ur): electric power produced from the energy of flowing water

**levees** (LEV-eez): raised river banks

**meteorologists** (mee-tee-ur-OL-oh-jists): scientists who study
the weather

**radar** (RAY-dar): a device that reflects radio waves off objects to
create a picture

**reservoirs** (REZ-uh-vwarz): lakes or ponds created by a dam

**satellites** (sat-uh-LITES): spacecraft that orbit the Earth and
send back photos or other information

**spillways** (SPIL-waze): channels used to move excess water
around a dam so it doesn't spill over the top

**storm surges** (STORM SUR-jez): a rush of water over the land
caused by low air pressure over the ocean

**tropical cyclones** (TRAH-pi-kuhl SYE-klonez): swirling storms
with high winds and heavy rainfall that occur in the tropical
parts of the world

**tsunami** (tsoo-NAH-mee): powerful ocean waves, usually
caused by an earthquake or volcanic eruption

**typhoons** (tye-FOONZ): tropical cyclones occuring in the
northwest Pacific Ocean

# Index

## Wesites to Visit

www.yourdiscovery.com/earth/water/flooding/index.shtml?cc=US

www.semo.state.ny.us/info/publicsafety/floodprepare.cfm

www.gohsep.la.gov/factsheets/floods.htm

www.noaawatch.gov/floods.php

www.simscience.org/cracks/intermediate/mintro.html

## About the Author

Joanne Mattern has written hundreds of nonfiction books for children. Nature, science, and natural disasters are some of her favorite topics, so FLOODS, DAMS, AND LEVEES was a very interesting book for her to write! Joanne grew up on the banks of the Hudson River in New York State and still lives in the area with her husband, four children, and many pets.